A HISTORY OF LAKE PLEASANT
STEUBEN COUNTY, INDIANA

Nancy Schall

We Authors llc
Tipp City, Ohio

Copyright © 2015 by Nancy Schall.

All rights reserved. No part of this publication may be reproduced, distributed or transmitted in any form or by any means, including photocopying, recording, or other electronic or mechanical methods, without the prior written permission of the publisher, except in the case of brief quotations embodied in critical reviews and certain other noncommercial uses permitted by copyright law. For permission requests, write to the publisher, addressed "Attention: Permissions Coordinator," at the address below.

We Authors llc
PMB #125 1841 W. Main St.
Troy, OH 45373
www.weauthors.net

Although the author and publisher have made every effort to ensure that the information in this book was correct at press time, the author and publisher do not assume and hereby disclaim any liability to any party for any loss, damage, or disruption caused by errors or omissions, whether such errors or omissions result from negligence, accident, or any other cause.

Book Layout ©2013 BookDesignTemplates.com.

Ordering Information:
Quantity sales. Special discounts are available on quantity purchases by corporations, associations, and others. For details, contact the "Special Sales Department" at the address above.

Chapter 13: History of the Dam written and contributed by Larry Bandelier.

Cover Design by Melinda Schall.
Cover Photos courtesy of Roger Schall, Phil Husband, Gene Hadley, Don Gillespie and Nancy Lehman. Digital format of black & white cover photos courtesy of Tammeron Jonesfrancis.

See acknowledgments, footnotes and photo captions for other contribution information, including interviews, photos, articles, letters, emails, and other documents donated or referenced in the creation of this book.

A History of Lake Pleasant - Steuben County, Indiana / Nancy Schall. -- 1st ed.
ISBN 978-0-9863497-3-7

Dedicated to the continued beauty and well-being of our home - Lake Pleasant.

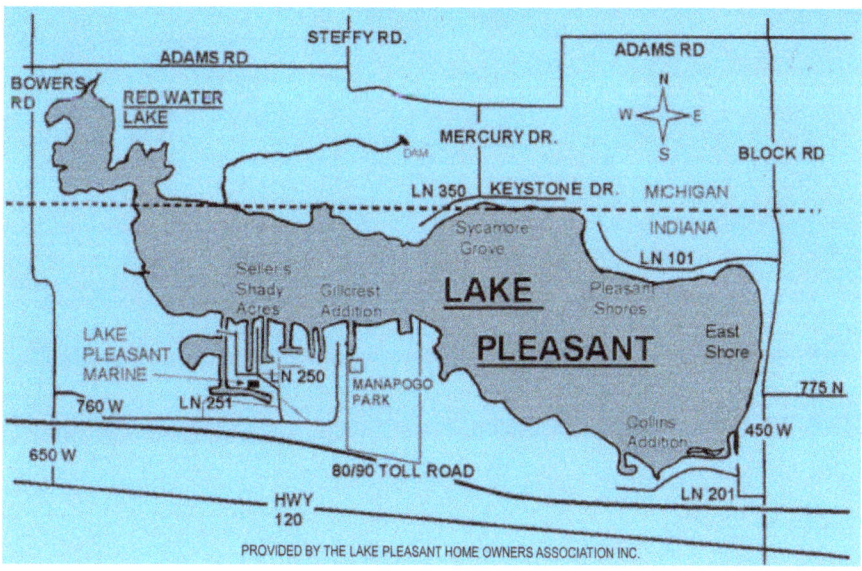

Contents

Title 1
Copyright 2
Dedication 3
Contents 5
Preface 7
Acknowledgments 9
Introduction 11
Lake Pleasant: 1800's 13
Red Water Lake: 1800's - Now 17
Bootleggers and Such: 1930's 19
Hobb's Resort: 1938 Through Early 1960's 21
About 1945 25
Early 1950's: Sherman's Addition 29
More from the 1950's on the Southwest Part of the Lake 33
Collins Addition, Southeast Shore Area: 1950's 39
The Willows Resort, East Shore: 1950's 43
The Palm Sunday Tornado of 1965 49
Manapogo Campground: 1960's 55
Pleasant Shores, Northeast Portion of the Lake: 1970's 59
History of the Dam 63
Conclusion 67

Preface

Information and photos in this book include anecdotes and documented history contributed by many lake residents as well as by interested community members. Much of this information was shared at the Reflections program sponsored by 101 Lakes Trust on Sunday, August 17, 2014. The program featured docents on pontoon boat tours who discussed points of interest and their development as the boats passed referenced locations. A narrated presentation followed at a catered dinner in Orland, a small town near Lake Pleasant.

Acknowledgments

The author would like to thank all who contributed to the collection of information, photos, and to the organization of these for this book (please see footnotes and/or photo captions throughout the book for details). In particular, Tammeron Jonesfrancis of Hell's Point Vineyards and Studio / Jonesfrancis Design and Nancy Bandelier were incredible assets as they worked together to identify, arrange, duplicate and label the photos used for the 101 Lakes Trust program. Tammeron then served as the digital photo technician for most of the photos included in this book. Thanks to Larry Bandelier for writing Chapter 13: History of the Dam. I am also extremely grateful to: John Kohl, copy editor; Melinda Schall, design editor and publisher at We Authors llc.; and the Lake Pleasant Homeowners Association Inc., who helped make it possible for present and future generations to appreciate the history of our "little piece of paradise."

Introduction

Lake Pleasant encompasses 424 acres and contains about 1,137 million gallons of water, with its deepest point measuring 52 feet. There is no public access, but there are two private access sites—one at Lake Pleasant Marine, and another at Manapogo Campground.[1]

A past president of the Lake Pleasant Homeowners Association, Janet Bohney, discovered an interesting fact from a website: Lake Pleasant is a registered place for seaplanes to land![2] It is assumed that this is because it is a long lake and because a former resident, Dr. Chupp, used to land his seaplane here.

---

[1] *Steuben County Lake Maps*. Steuben County Surveyor's Office, 1991.
[2] "Water Landing Directory." Seaplane Pilots Association. 2012. Accessed 2014. www.seaplanes.org.

CHAPTER ONE

Lake Pleasant: 1800's

The second oldest historical document gathered at the point of publication of this history begins with an article from a small book that was published for the centennial in Orland in 1934. Published on August 24, 1934, by the Orland Centennial Committee and the Steuben Printing Company of Angola, Indiana, the book sold for 25 cents. The barber in Orland in 2014, Kim Norton, found the following article and donated it for the Reflections program described in the preface of this book.

INDIANS WERE HERE: 1800'S

In those days the Potawatomi Indians were all over the country, as this region was their hunting grounds. Although they caused the settlers some concern, they were quite peaceable when sober. They were ruled by the just and wise chief, Baw Beese, who usually resided in Branch County. The Indians frequently appropriated for themselves property belonging to the settlers. Rev. Holdstock, a circuit rider, who preached in the county about 1839-40, planned to be married in Orland on June 15, 1840. Just before that date the Indians stole his horse. This did not prevent the wedding, however, for he walked to Angola, got his license, and walked to Orland in time for the ceremony. His salary at that time was $40 a year and he had thirty appointments to fill.

Henry Depue settled in 1835 on what is now the home of Dexter Wilder, east of Orland. The following summer, one of his hogs strayed away. Taking his gun, he started out to look for the missing animal. In his journeyings he came to the south shore of Lake Pleasant. Looking across the water, he saw some Indians had killed his hog and were dragging it to Hickory Point, some thirty rods away. A sandbar extends across the lake at this place. Mr. Depue ran out on the bar and shot at them, but missed his mark. He began at once to reload, but in his excitement he dropped the gun into the water. He was now beside himself with rage. He picked up his now useless gun and started across the sandbar as fast as he could in water three feet deep. As he neared the Indians one of them shot him in the arm with an arrow, then they all ran away. Mr. Depue bound up his arm and hurried to the home of his brother, John, where the deep wound was properly dressed. His brother, being on the best of terms with the Indians, induced him to accompany him to their camp, where they had a talk and smoked the pipe of peace. Henry often said it was the toughest smoke he ever had as there was no love in his heart for an Indian. The pipe of peace was usually filled with a mixture of red willow bark and tobacco, kept in a sack for use as occasion demanded. The Indian name for the mixture was Kin-na-ra-nick. About 1838, the Indians were removed to a reservation in the Far West. Heartbroken at leaving their homes, many found their way back and it was several years later before all had left the country never to return.[3]

---

[3] "Indians Were Here," Orland Centennial Committee, Steuben Printing Company, Angola, IN, August 24, 1934.

Chief Pokagon
(photo on the left)
"A correct likeness of Chief Simon Pokagon in his tribal attire as he appeared at the Chicago World's Fair on Chicago Day, October 9, 1893, as painted by M.O. Whitney. Being an invited guest of the city on that day, the old veteran rang the new liberty bell for the first time, and was honored by addressing the throng in behalf of his race."[4]

(Note from the author – Chief Pokagon was a famous chief of the Potawatomi whose name is honored by the name of our local Pokagon State Park.)

Native American Warrior Coe-Coosh, or The Hog, by Paul Kane
(photo on the right)
"The clothing and hair of this warrior from Wisconsin reflect styles common among the more northern Potawatomis. Courtesy Stark Museum of Art, Orange, Texas."[5]

---

[4] Munger, Lynn. "Chief Pokagon." Fremont, IN: Potawatomi Museum. April 2015.
[5] Edmunds, David R. "The Potawatomis, Keepers of the Fire." In The Civilization of the American Indian Series, 61. First ed. Vol. 145. University of Oklahoma Press, Publishing Division of the University, 1978.

Algonquian Summer House
"A traditional type of dwelling used by the Potawatomi and other tribes in the Old Northwest. Courtesy National Archives."[6]

Fish Scaling Tool (left side)
"The tool on the left was used by the Potawatomi. Held with the scooped side away from the palm of ones hand, it still can be used to scale fish."

Arrowhead (middle)
"This tiny arrowhead was found in the shallow water on the east end of Lake Pleasant. Lynn "Doc" Munger, local historian, describes it as a type used by the Potawatomi Indians to hunt fish and birds."[7]

(Quarter included to show scale.)

---

[6] Edmunds, "The Potawatomis, Keepers of the Fire," 60.
[7] Munger, Lynn. "Arrowhead and Fish Scaling Tools." Fremont, IN: Potawatomi Museum. April 2015.

CHAPTER TWO

Red Water Lake: 1800's - Now

According to the current property owner and the aforementioned story of the Potawatomi Indians, these Native Americans did, indeed, live in the still undeveloped area of Lake Pleasant always known as "Red Water." It gets its name from the tannin in the bottom of the weed-covered bottom, which casts a reddish color during much of the year. Before the 1950's, there was a huckleberry marsh in this area, where this rare type of wild blueberries was found, due to the below 6.4 pH level in the soil. However, the pH changed as time passed and the huckleberries disappeared.[8]

It has been reported that there is an Indian mound on the property, and artifacts have been found representing the Potawatomi and probably groups before them, according to the owner of the land and senior citizens from the area who remember hearing about the finds. Lynn "Doc" Munger mentions trapping turtles in Red Water back in the 1930s, a practice which at that time was quite lucrative, and selling them for food. Aside from the largely unknown history of this section of Lake Pleasant, its natural beauty attracts tourists and fishermen, families and sweethearts, well into the fall.

---

[8] Munger, Lynn, interview by author, April 17, 2015.

Present Day Red Water in the Fall
(Both, courtesy of Roger Schall)

CHAPTER THREE

Bootleggers and Such: 1930's

Local historian, Doc Munger, tells of a small store on the east end of the lake run by a family named Musser, who also ran a restaurant. The business property was sold several times. The last owners that Munger remembers were Eva and Bob Paul. Dan and Sue Schoenbein bought the property in 1955 and later developed a small resort that they called "The Willows." (See Chapter 9, "The Willows Resort, East Shore: 1950's.")

At the same time, two bootleggers were in operation on the extreme northeast corner of the lake. Prohibition was in effect, and a man known as Dad Chambers owned a shack-like home from which illegal home brew was sold. Another bootlegger operated just across the road (County Road 450W) and a couple of houses south. Doc Munger remembers drinking illegal liquor at Chambers' place with an older cousin when the former was only 15.

Olinger Cottage
Formerly Bootlegger's Cottage / "Dad" Chambers' Place
(Courtesy of Tammeron Jonesfrancis)

During the 1930's-40's, Doc Munger remembers trapping turtles to sell for food in the northwest adjoining lake known as Red Water. Selling turtles then was a lucrative hobby, and the turtles from Red Water could be huge. He also mentions in his letter that early landowners on the north shore were Hank Merriman and Chauncey Unrue, and that pike fishing was a very popular sport, with the lake abundantly filled with pike.[9]

---

[9] Munger, Lynn, letter to 101 Lakes Trust, August 2014.

CHAPTER FOUR

Hobb's Resort: 1938 Through Early 1960's

The oldest developed section of Lake Pleasant was once known as Hobb's Resort but is now referred to as Sycamore Grove. A Mr. and Mrs. Hobalusa developed a group of fishing cottages called "Hobb's Resort" and also ran a store in back of their own residence, which is still remembered today as a place where children enjoyed buying penny candy while their

Hobb's Cottage (Courtesy of Phil Husband and Gene Hadley)

parents shopped for basic supplies. The cottages were very simple, with some having no drywall and containing telephone pole crossbeams for studs (complete with creosote odor), bare live wires in the walls, added bathrooms which were plumbing nightmares, added showers in bedrooms, etc.[10]

According to families who owned land along Lake Pleasant in the early years, people from the fishing camps and other lake properties used to spear carp up to 40 inches long at several places on the lake, along with catching the pike that Mr. Munger mentioned in his letter and other species of popular fish such as catfish, perch, blue gill, bass, and crappie.

The area where Hobb's Resort was now contains mostly remodeled homes, of which a few are quite elaborate. There are still about three or four that resemble the earlier cabins and retain their charm.

One of the cottages today which maintains its old fashioned appearance and charm. (Courtesy of DeLeah Kohl)

---

[10] Bohney, Janet, interview by author, May 10, 2014.

Hobb's Resort
(Courtesy of Phil Husband and Gene Hadley)

The Candy Store at Hobalusa's
(Courtesy of Gene Hadley)

CHAPTER FIVE

About 1945

Tidbits of history come from Don Gillespie, whose family has owned his place across County Road 450 since 1945, when his grandfather, John Ackerman, who had fished on Lake George for many years, was attracted to Lake Pleasant by its outstanding sunsets. These influenced his hobby of photography and led him to purchase a lot.

In about 1948, Don's Grandpa John and two neighbors had dredging done in front of their lots, and then used the dredged material to fill in the front lots from County Road 450 to the lake. John fished Lake Pleasant and also Hog Lake (now Barton Lake), which at that time had an island and no cottages.

While he was managing Portland Lumber and Supply in Portland, IN, John had six twin-hulled boats built, using 3/4" cedar wood—making them very heavy, but stable for fishing. As a boy, Don got the chore of filling

and soaking the boat that John kept at Lake Pleasant with water on weekends so that it would not shrink. When the family returned the next time, he had to bale that water out so that the boat could be used. During the Palm Sunday tornado of 1965, two of the twin-hulled boats were driven by the storm into trees back on Hog Lake.

Lamprey Eel
(All photos this chapter, courtesy of Don Gillespie)

Don also tells of a creature found in the lake, which was identified by a biologist as a lamprey eel.[11] Perhaps this relates to another story from even longer ago, which was in the May 27, 1912 *Herald Republican* newspaper of Angola, IN, and republished under the heading "80 years ago," in 1992. The legend of a sea serpent apparently originated in 1912 but is still referenced by local folks today.

---

[11] Gillespie, Don, interview by author, July 2014.

The article reads:

> Orville Goodale fished one day last week on Lake Pleasant, east of Orland, and had for his guide an old-time fisherman by the name of Peter Casebeer. This is a beautiful lake, and among other things is noted for a huge snake that has been seen there from time to time for many years. The first to see the snake, so far as the memory of the man goes, was the same Peter Casebeer and his wife, who were fishing on the lake. They did not see the head or tail of the snake, but several feet of its body appeared above the water. The body looked to be six inches or so in diameter, and judging from the commotion it made in the water, Mr. Casebeer is certain it was twenty feet in length. Mrs. Casebeer was so frightened that she was sick with nervous trouble for two or more weeks.
>
> Later the monster was seen by Jacob Rubeley and a Mr. Blaine and others, some declaring it to be thirty feet long. As it had not been seen for a few years, Mr. Goodale ventured on the lake and came off safe and sound.[12] [13]

Another article about the sea monster may predate the 1912 report above. Ernest Neutz, grandfather of 95-year-old Lynn "Doc" Munger (cited previously), wrote the following paragraph about his experience with the creature.

> One time I went fishing with the Nettleman boys on Lake Pleasant. We fished on the north side of the lake along the rushes. We caught lots of blue gill and large perch. When we were fishing, we saw something coming toward the boat all the time. It looked like a big saw log with a big knot on the end. The small fish seemed to follow it up. When it got close enough so we could see it plain, it opened its mouth big enough to take the boat right in. So I turned the boat around and, Oh my god, how we did row for shore. We reached the shore all right. I gave all the fish to the Nettleman boys. Well, I never went to fish on the north shore anymore. So people who do fish on Lake Pleasant are warned to always fish on the south side of the lake and look out for the big sea monster.[14]

---

[12] *The Herald Republican*, May 27, 1912, Local Interest Stories Section.
[13] "80 Years Ago." *The Herald Republican*, May 27, 1992.
[14] Neutz, Ernest. 2002. "Nevada Mills Sea Monster Described by Neutz." In Munger, Lynn, *The History of Nevada Mills*. Fremont, IN: Potawatomi Museum, p.53. Fremont, IN, 2002.

CHAPTER SIX

Early 1950's: Sherman's Addition

Most of the development of different sections of the land around Lake Pleasant occurred after 1950, and some was connected to the coming of the turnpike, which divided farms and caused owners to sell sections. However, the area now referred to as the Sherman Addition has some distinct differences in early stories, not reflecting the farmers' perspective.

In October 1952, Hugh and Bob Ford owned a car dealership in Portland, Indiana. A man needed a car and traded his lake property on Lake Pleasant for that car. The Fords started in a prefabricated building that was relocated from Ball State University's "married housing." Their walls were held together with steel cable, and there was no indoor plumbing. They hauled water from neighbors who had a deeper well and a pump in their front lot. The children of Hugh Ford still own and enjoy the remodeled cottage at its original lake location.

Original Ford Cottage

**Hank Newhouse, a Ford Family Friend,
Fishing in Early Sherman's Addition
(Both, courtesy of the Ford family)**

Many of the north shore places replaced older ones or were built on empty lots back in the 1950's. The Fords' neighbor, Mr. Fox, was on the lake for years before they arrived and told them he paid $35 for his front lot and $25 for the back lots. But when the Fords arrived, the lots were going for around $250. The Fords remember frog gigging and turtle hunting in a little pond back behind the road on the north shore. At that time, the lake was considered too small for skiing; fishing was the pastime.

The Ford siblings using the lake cottages in 2014 remember when, in 1964-65, the state laws changed so that the channels in the lake were counted as lake acreage. After that, skiing was allowed. The previous 10 mph speed limit on the lake became a thing of the past, and fishermen had to watch out for speed boats and skiers. At first there was a sort of gentleman's agreement, or "courtesy law," which gave the fishermen the use of the lake until 9 am and again after 5 pm. As the lake has become more populated, this "law" is no longer observed.[15]

---

[15] Ford, Jeanna, interview by author, July 1, 2014.

CHAPTER SEVEN

More from the 1950's on the Southwest Part of the Lake

Several people report that, to the west of the Red Water area and round the bend, there is a fence in the lake. It is presumably from Kenneth Sellers' farm, which was divided by the coming of the turnpike in the early 50's. Lance Dafforn, whose family has been on the lake from the 60's, stated that the shoreline of the lake has changed due to erosion and changing water levels. The lake has crept inland, possibly resulting in covering up the farm fence. Lance estimated that the lake used to be about 120 feet away from the shoreline that we see today,[16] though others disagree the lakeshore has changed so much.

According to Lilah Sellers, daughter-in-law of Mr. Kenneth Sellers, and early maps and abstracts from property owners, Mr. Sellers did develop the area now known as "Sellers Shady Shores" in the early 1950's, when the turnpike divided his farm. The channels were dug in 1953-56.[17]

Mr. Sellers then also built the marine to service Lake Pleasant residents and their boating needs. Floyd Yerington bought it in about 1971 and added basic grocery items with candy, ice cream, pop, and beer. Steve Daler purchased the marine in 1996 and still runs it today (2014) with his son, Tracy.

Kenneth Sellers occupied one cottage very near the marine and rented out two others. According to his daughter-in-law, Lilah Sellers, he always

---

[16] Dafforn, Lance, interview by author, June 24, 2014.
[17] Sellers, Lilah, interview by author, June 2014.

Above: Original Sellers Cottage (Courtesy of DeLeah Kohl)

Left: Original Lehman Cottage (Courtesy of Nancy Lehman)

wanted his children to have homes or cottages here, but they were farmers and were too busy to enjoy lake places. He and his family graciously donated the beach area to the Sellers Shady Shores Association to be used and protected by property owners in this section.

Cottage owners in the early Sellers years had annual volleyball tournaments, a tradition that was carried on for many years. From about 2004-2014, the Sellers Shady Shores Association has hosted an annual picnic with hot dogs and other food, also providing children's games and corn-hole tournaments for all to enjoy.

Volleyball During Sellers Picnic

Mr. Sellers had most of the channels dug so that land could be supplied for cottages. But one channel, a T-shaped channel on the eastern edge of the area, was dug by the property owners south of it to drain a boggy area and to cut down on mosquitos.

T-shaped Channel (Both, courtesy of Carole Diehm)

Interesting memories from Sellers' Shady Shores include:
- a dance floor where sock hops were held.
- a shuffle board court to the south and east of the original Sellers cottage.
- a diving board and slide on the beach, placed there by some of the original families in the Sellers Addition.

**Diving Board
(Courtesy of Carole Diehm)**

The cement base of the diving board was finally removed in 2013. Families still in the area remember even a high dive, made from a windmill, with an area deep enough for diving dug out under the board by cottage owners.[18] This deeper area is now a fishing hole accessible from the shore.

Fishing is good in an undeveloped part of the lake just south of Sellers and the campground, and for the adventurous, boats can carefully maneuver through reeds and cattails to find what some families call "The Marl Pit."

---
[18] Diehm, Carole, letter to author, July 2014.

Others entertain their children with the idea of a "Monster" pit, since it is so isolated. Marl was mined from most of the area lakes and was used for various purposes.

Dan Schoenbein, from the east end of the lake years ago, said that marl was used to make gunpowder, but a local historian, Jeanne Whitcomb, said it was used (perhaps also) as an alternative to lime to put on the fields to alter alkalinity. Her father created a device to spread the marl on fields, saving farmers the work of shoveling it out of a truck and raking it out by hand. Interestingly, the fish caught in the marl pit often have different coloring—usually a dark bluish-black.[19]

---

[19] Whitcomb, Jean, interview by author, May 15, 2014.

CHAPTER EIGHT

Collins Addition, Southeast Shore Area: 1950's

Frank Collins originally owned the farm that he developed into the lake properties now called the Collins addition after the turnpike was finished in about 1954. Frank sold the lots for $500 between the late 1950's and the early 1960's.

In 2014, Ron Spade, a local retired Department of Natural Resources employee and Frank's grandson, still lived at the intersection of County Road 450W and State Route 120. He told about Dennisons and another neighbor digging the channel in front of their places through the ice, placing the dirt on the high spot that now has become an island. They also later dug a channel just to the west. Ron's brother, Herbert, lived in Orland when he built a shack of sorts, put it on skids, and placed it on the last lot his grandfather had to sell, where Beams have a summer place now at the end of the road into the development. This was not legal, since Spades had no water or way to take care of waste, but the local county officials let them be since another group was also "camping" in a well house. Eventually the other group got very rowdy with parties, etc., and one day Herbert came to find a red notice on his shack. He could no longer use it.[20] The shack is still there in 2014, behind the A-frame at 340 Lane 201, according to Sue Stillwell.[21] [22]

---

[20] Spade, Ron, interview by author, August 2014.
[21] Spade, Herbert, interview by author, August 2014.
[22] Stillwell, Sue, interview by author, August 2014.

Chris Yesh told those researching the history of Lake Pleasant about a spring at the east end of the island that has water about twenty degrees below the temperature of the rest of the lake—so cold that one's feet get numb quickly if put into it. The blue cottage near the spring, on the peninsula north of the island, was the first cottage built south of the Willows resort. The Willows resort was established in 1955, as Mr. Collins began developing the Collins Addition.

One of the earliest cottages after the Willows was established. This cottage looks almost exactly as it did when built. (Courtesy of DeLeah Kohl)

A small controversy upset neighbors in the Collins addition and was also described to the researchers by Chris Yesh. In the 1960s, a local property owner began to dig a channel so he could flood lake water into it and then build a trailer park on the surrounding property. Neighbors did not want this and went to court to stop the development.

More-recent history from the Collins Addition includes a tragic fire which destroyed an already remodeled home late in October, 2010. Since the fire occurred after the summer season, no one was home. Chris and Patricia Yesh had to rebuild once more, and today their home is one of the most beautiful residences on the lake.[23]

Yesh Home After the Fire

**Yesh Home Today
(Both, courtesy of Chris Yesh)**

---

[23] Yesh, Chris, interview by author, July 2014.

CHAPTER NINE

The Willows Resort, East Shore: 1950's

The group of cottages around a small private beach on the east end of Lake Pleasant was once known as "the Willows" and was almost totally hidden by large, beautiful willow trees. The property was originally part of 92.28 acres purchased in 1835 for $300. 2.04 acres of that property were later passed through various owners. Then Dan and Sue Schoenbein bought it from a Mr. Paul in 1955 for $8000.[24] They developed the Willows resort and were dearly loved by many LPHOA members who once rented there but now have places of their own.

THE WILLOWS RESORT – LAKE PLEASANT, IND.

---

[24] Steuben County IN. Property Abstract, Tract 1,2,3, Sec. 18 Jamestown Township, 38N. October. 1955.

THE WILLOWS RESORT – LAKE PLEASANT IND.

(Postcards, previous page and above, courtesy of Nancy Lehman)

Sue probably taught at least 50-70 children to swim, while Dan kept them in line with a rather gruff demeanor—then helped Sue slip candy into their bags as they packed up to go home. Dan showed pictures of the "ginormous" fish he caught in Florida during the winter and told of his days trapping around Lake Pleasant.

**Dan Schoenbein
(Courtesy of Erna Schuller)**

Paul Baldwin, 90, was one of those who rented from Dan and Sue and even one year from the owners before them. Paul tells of a reddish colored cottage down closer to the lake which had been an ice house and was insulated with sawdust. Although he added that his family didn't like it much because it drew mice. They started renting in about 1954, and there were no other cottages besides the Willows on this part of County Road 450W.

**Former Ice House Cottage
(Courtesy of Erna Schuller)**

Later, the Baldwin's rented the big, two-story cottage for $30 a week. That was too much for his family, so they went in with another family. There was no indoor plumbing; they washed clothes in spring water—including diapers—and hung everything out on the line.

Early Cottages at the Willows
(Courtesy of Erna Schuller)

The first cottage built after Baldwin started renting was a blue one on "the peninsula" just south of Willows. Looking North from the Willows, one can see evidence in early pictures of outhouses placed right near the shore, something that would not be tolerated today.

Example of Outhouses near the Lake
(Courtesy of Don Gillespie)

Within the next 10-12 years, Paul saw a cabin built on this end of the lake for sale for $5000.[25] Sue Schoenbein's sister, Erna, lived at the Willows with her husband, Walt, and in August of 2014 provided researchers with photos and slides from Dan and Sue's days at the Willows. These cottages are now (2014) owned by Rozanne and Shirley Hallman and are still being rented for vacation weeks by descendants and friends of some vacationers of earlier years.

---

[25] Baldwin, Paul, interview with author, June 2014.

CHAPTER TEN

The Palm Sunday Tornado of 1965

The Willows and several properties to the north of there, plus the Collins Addition developed at the time, were destroyed in 1965 by the largest tornado ever to strike Indiana. It wreaked destruction over twenty

Collins Shoreline
(Courtesy of Erna Schuller)

miles in a three-hour time period on Palm Sunday that year. Sadly, Dan and Sue Schoenbein had just paid off their mortgage for the Willows the year before and had no insurance.

The following is a first-hand report on the tornado's effect on the Willows area from Erna Schuller, now living in Tennessee with her husband and daughter. This was her response to: "Where were you when it hit?" The clarifications in parentheses are from the writer recording this history.

Sue and Dan (Schoenbein) were in Florida and we got a call at a friend's house from Clara Young that a tornado hit their place. We started out EARLY from home with a borrowed pickup and when we were close to their resort...we saw the chicken barn...it was a long building and the roof came down on the chickens...Dead and living chickens were under the roof...and when they raised the roof that day...there were chickens all over the place and it was full of eggs!!! Then we saw a sport car all twisted up in a tree and a man was hanging out of the door...dead...and already stripped of rings and watch!! Then we came over the hill and both of us screamed...it was a sight that was unbelievable!! Piles of rubbish...on top of the collapsed house was a toilet ...intact...and the divan. Trees were stripped of bark and an aluminum boat twisted around a tree that was stripped of the bark and most branches. It was as if a giant uprooted the LARGE tree...the huge tree left a hole in the ground that was waist deep...The looters arrived at dawn and Walt scared them off saying he was willing to shoot...we didn't have a gun....

By then the neighbor was there with a big truck and other neighbors from Michigan helped us fill the truck and take it to his chicken coops for storage. We worked until it was too dark. Then started again in the morning. We slowly got to the basement, thru the smashed up house and there a beam lay across the candy case...it was unhurt!!! I found Sue's silverware, etc. and handed them up to the neighbor...a cupboard was intact and I salvaged what I could handing it to Rubley...who stayed all day again with us and helped fill his storage places to the brim!!! One cottage survived because of fallen trees, etc. The place where the big one was had been cleaned off and looked like the floor had been scrubbed....

On and on...I could go...But! when I lifted the couch seat up...their silver ware was all there...protected...and some pictures, etc. We found their canning jars in the field across the road. Sue put paper inside and screwed the lids on...there wasn't a lid to be found and the jars...intact!!! Many weird things...#8 (one of the cottages) blew into the lake...our kids and others dragged bed springs out of the lake for a long time...had to wear shoes but no cut feet...most wasn't sharp edges from landing in the water ....Sorry...I do ramble on. Many stories of people helping...actually staying in trailers, etc.[26]

East Shore Looking North

**Schoenbein Property
(Both, courtesy of Erna Schuller)**

---

[26] Schuller, Erna, email message to the author, July 2014.

**Sue Schoenbein
(Courtesy of Erna Schuller)**

Doc Munger was a friend of the Schoenbeins who came to check on the damage after the tornado and was there when Sue's diamond ring was discovered in the rubble. Imagine the likelihood of such a discovery in so much devastation![27]

Another story of the tornado damage comes from a close relative of Kenneth Sellers, who developed the Sellers Shady Shores on the southwest portion of the lake. Although Kenneth's home was not on the lake, the story of his residence adjacent to the lake and just east of the Willows area is interesting to include, historically.

At the time of the tornado, Kenneth Sellers and his wife, Gladys, had been living in their lake place but were still vacationing in Florida. Their daughter, Jane, and her husband, Dave Coler, lived in "the home place," Kenneth's farmhouse on St. Rt. 120, just east of Lake Pleasant, but had traveled to Florida to bring the Sellers back from their winter vacation there.

---

[27] Munger, Lynn, interview by author, April 17, 2015.

While Jane and David were gone, Larry and Diane Penix (Coler's daughter and her husband), with their six-month-old baby girl, were taking care of the farm.

The day of the tornado, a couple of Diane's brothers and a sister-in-law were in the farmhouse, and they were gathered on the covered back porch, cleaning fish. As the wind increased, a tree came crashing down. Suddenly, a loud, train-like noise came through the kitchen window in back of them. A brother tried to get to the basement, but the rest of the family did not escape in time and ended up in the debris of the home, which was destroyed. Amazingly, none were seriously injured, although all went to the hospital. The brother who had attempted to get to the cellar suffered a broken sternum; the rest, according to the doctor, had "barnyard injuries."

When the family came to their senses, they were covered in dirt and debris. One brother thought to start the car so they could go for help, but then they realized the roads would all be blocked by damaged trees and other homes. Slightly disoriented, they left the car running and decided to walk to a neighbor's home, but the neighbor was not there. Finding a towel at the neighbor's, Diane wiped the blood coming from her husband's lacerated head. The family came out of the neighbor's house to find a sheriff's car in the drive. In the car were Elmer Molter and Gary Jacob, men who knew the family but did not recognize them with all the scrapes, blood, and dirt on them. (Diane says they were so dirty that her doctor made her shower before he examined her at the hospital.)

Sadly, after the tragic destruction of the Sellers' home place, looters came. Gary Jacob provided assistance to the family by staying near the homestead to prevent their attempts to benefit from the disaster.[28]

---

[28] Penix, Diane, interview by author, April 17, 2015.

"Nothing left but hope." – Dan Schoenbein
(Courtesy of Erna Schuller)

CHAPTER ELEVEN

Manapogo Campground: 1960's

Manapogo Campground was originally established in 1965 and was owned by Lance Dafforn's father, Derald Dafforn. He started it with only ten campsites and one water spigot. Rumors abound regarding the "campground wars," but details were not provided to researchers. Lance referenced the "wars" in a recent conversation, and long-time folks around Lake Pleasant remember that there was much resistance to the coming of a campground to the lake.

Don Gillespie and Paul Baldwin, who have been on the lake for more than fifty years, remember boating past the woods years before the 60's, when there were just a few campers, and hearing the shots of people squirrel hunting there. Only 9-horsepower motors were allowed on the lake in those days.

Manapogo is now owned by Mr. and Mrs. John West. Most of the campsites there are seasonal, and many families are there as often as cottage owners are. Wests and their staff have made many contributions to help the Lake Pleasant Homeowners Association, including helping with weed control and annual fireworks and providing major assistance with on-going dam cleanup, annual trash pickup, and a recent fish-attractor project.

Present Day Manapogo Campground – Beach Fun
(Both, courtesy of Sue West – Manapogo Campground Owner)

A HISTORY OF LAKE PLEASANT | 57

Kid Favorites: Carol and Ice Cream

Manapogo Campground Playground
(Both, courtesy of Sue West – Manapogo Campground Owner)

CHAPTER TWELVE

Pleasant Shores, Northeast Portion of the Lake: 1970's

In 1837, President Martin Van Buren authorized the sale of 154.75 acres to William Martin, who retained ownership until 1910, when a parcel of the land was sold to Chauncey Unrue. Upon Unrue's death in 1960, the property went to his son, Robert, who in turn had the area along the northeast shore (Lane 101) platted into 16 lots. All 16 lots were sold, and the majority of the homes were built in the 1970's and later.[29]

During the early periods of development, roads were so poorly defined that they contributed to this story: Phil Husband was building his cottage and had ordered a load of drywall from the lumber yard in Angola to be delivered on a Saturday morning. He waited and waited, no drywall—and in the day of no cell phones, he had to go to a pay phone on a drive going back to Barton Lake to call the lumber yard. After "polite" discussion about the non-delivered goods, the lumber company told the owner they had put the drywall in the garage of the house being constructed, since it was open. Unfortunately, they had delivered the drywall to the wrong place.

People along Lane 101 in Pleasant Shores used to have fun Fourth of July parades, when they dressed up crazily, put flags on lawnmowers, and used horns and rattles to create a loud, festive spirit, according to current resident Phil Husband. Phil also tells about Vern Kiess, who drove his four-wheeler

---

[29] Steuben County IN. Property Abstract, Ln 101 Lake Pleasant, Pleasant Shores Lot #2, Chris Stephen. May 2014.

with his wife wearing a very large, long yellow T-shirt that said "Vern's Girl" on it. People from County Road 450 came to watch and wave, while others on boats blew their horns from the water.

Stories are also told of "Dewey's Dilly," a cottage on the east edge of Pleasant Shores, in which apparently resided a winter fun-loving family whose parents and three children zoomed across the lake in 4-5 snowmobiles at a time. In the 70's, this was a rather unusual and very noisy sight. [30]

An observable trace of the history of Pleasant Shores is a distinctly elevated ridge at the back of the cottages. This is the result of dirt being pulled down to the edge of the lake to fill in what was once boggy ground so that it could be usable lakefront property.

Shoreline in 1972
(Courtesy of Phil Husband)

The Ridge Today
(Courtesy of Nancy Bandelier)

---

[30] Husband, Phil, interview by author, June 2014.

Pleasant Shores Shoreline Today
(Courtesy of Nancy Schall)

CHAPTER THIRTEEN

History of the Dam

WRITTEN BY LARRY BANDELIER

Around the mid 1980's, during the annual property owners' association meeting, a local property owner (Al Deininger) interrupted the meeting. All excited, he said something had to be done before the properties along County Road 450W were flooded. (We had experienced a very rainy spring.) He was asking for volunteers to cut through the reeds and cattails on the northwest side of the lake and make a channel to a creek in Michigan. This would allow the water to get away faster, since it wouldn't be slowed by the cattails.

At this time there was no outlet from the lake except through the wetlands. Several people with shovels and gas-powered tools volunteered and cut this channel. (I don't know how long this took them.) This was done without any permits or permission, neither from the Indiana nor the Michigan Department of Natural Resources.

Soon the water level of the lake began dropping. However, the channel they dug allowed the lake to drop lower than anyone intended, and it kept dropping, making it difficult for many to get their boats away from their docks. As memory serves me, the channel was about 3 feet deep, due to the fact the cattails were actually floating above the surface of the lake bottom. When they were removed, the water had no buffer to keep from draining the lake down to that level.

The owner of Manapogo Campground (Derald Dafforn) was concerned about the safety of those swimming and diving from the swimming platform at the campground beach. He petitioned the Michigan Department of Natural Resources (DNR) for a permit to construct a temporary dam structure in the channel in order to stop the outflow. Since he owned the property in Michigan through which the channel had been cut, Michigan granted him the permit.

He then asked for volunteers to haul sandbags filled with sand and concrete mix to stack in the channel in order to stop the outflow of lake water. Around 8-10 men and boys spent 5-6 hours filling the bags, transporting them to the site, stacking the bags, and securing them with reinforcing steel bars. The dam height was brought up to the base level of the surrounding cattails. The water soaked through the bags, mixed with the concrete, and created a solid structure.

Soon news of the dam spread. Someone notified the Indiana DNR and told them that the campground owner had illegally built a dam on the lake. Without checking with the campground owner, a member of the Indiana DNR trespassed onto the Michigan property and, using dynamite, blew up the dam.

After that, the Lake Association, along with the campground owner, proposed a permanent channel with a permanent dam to control the lake level. A straight route from Prairie Creek in Michigan to the main body of Lake Pleasant through the cattails and solid land was proposed. This would go through both Indiana and Michigan properties. However, the Indiana landowner refused to allow the channel through his property.

The Michigan property owner, who was also the campground owner, donated his land for the project. However, this required a channel over a half mile in length to be dug, so that it could remain entirely on his property. This channel was done at a much greater expense to the Lake Association members than if it could have used the Indiana property.

After the channel was dug, a large steel culvert pipe was placed in the channel so the water flowed through it. Then a steel plate was welded across the front of the culvert to act as a permanent water-level control point. The lake level was arrived at by a consensus of property owners and the Indiana DNR.

The permanent lake level was officially established on April 11, 1986, by the Steuben County Circuit Court, at 961.5 feet above sea level. This worked well for a couple of years, until one winter the ice built up in front of the culvert and pushed it away. This created quite an emergency, as the lake level dropped quickly. Permits for another dam were received from Michigan, and money was loaned to the association for the project, interest free, by one of the lake's property owners.

This new dam was made entirely from two rows of steel pilings driven in rows two feet apart and filled in between with concrete. The sides of the dam extended several feet away from both sides of the channel into solid ground. This structure has remained since January, 1990. However, it has required work from many volunteers over the past several years to keep beavers from preventing the water from flowing over the dam. [31]

The Dam Today (Courtesy of Roger Schall)

---

[31] Bandelier, Larry. "History of the Dam." June 10, 2014. Article, Reflections Program from 101 Lakes Trust, Orland, August 17, 2014.

Added to Mr. Bandelier's report are a few anecdotal memories from contributors to this research project. Several lake residents today remember kayaking or motoring through the channel to enjoy viewing and photographing nature. People tell of amazing nature photos taken of deer, bullfrogs, raccoons, and a variety of flowers and birds. Roger and Nancy Schall used to travel through it with their family until it finally was too weedy to navigate. Their excursions started very early in the morning and yielded many precious memories and photos, including the following one taken by their son Michael Schall as part of his 4H photography project in 1994.

"Deer at Dawn"
(Courtesy of Michael Schall)

CHAPTER FOURTEEN

Conclusion

This concludes the anecdotal and historical records acquired by volunteers from the Lake Pleasant Homeowners Association after they were made aware of the fact that there was no written history available at local libraries. We would like people to be aware of this little piece of paradise and to appreciate its story. Many people contributed to this endeavor, and we are extremely grateful. The effort was undertaken as a result of participation in the 101 Lakes Trust annual program, "Reflections," held on Lake Pleasant on August 17, 2014.

ABOUT THE SPONSOR AND AUTHORS

This book is published thanks to the Lake Pleasant Homeowners Association, whose purpose (according to its Constitution and By Laws) is to protect the quality of the lake, enhance its natural attributes, and conserve and perpetuate the property-at-large of Lake Pleasant. In 2015, LPHOA Inc. President, Nancy Schall, asked the Board of Officers and Directors to approve sharing information and photos she gathered and arranged as articles in chronological order in the form of a book. The board agreed to have books be made available to lake association members and their families. Nancy also asked that copies be given free of charge to area libraries, who currently had no written history of the lake in their files, and to a few major contributors to the endeavor who are not currently property owners at Lake Pleasant. Articles in the book were written by Mrs. Nancy Schall and Mr. Larry Bandelier. Both are year round residents of the Lake and wish to preserve its heritage. Photos and information were contributed by many interested area volunteers.